Prayer Shawl Encouragement

By

Karen Doolaard

Prayer Shawl Encouragement

1. Praying it Forward.
2. How Marvelous
3. Giving Thanks .
4. Jonah Days
5. Survive or Thrive
6. Letting Go
7. Praying Victoriously
8. Rest in Peace
9. The Courage of Your Conviction
10. Forgetting What is Behind
11. Peace
12. What is your gift?
13. Feeding on His Word
14. Whiter than Snow
15. Sing to the Lord
16. Kind Words
17. Calling on Him
18. The Joy of Your Salvation
19. Dedicated
20. Hell is for Real
21. Great is Thy Faithfulness
22. Eyes
23. Hurry
24. God's Names
25. Religious or Spiritual
26. A "Can Do" Attitude
27. And It Came to Pass
28. Be Nice
29. Yarn Reproducing
30. Passing Through
31. Where is Your Mission Field?
32. Same Old, Same Old
33. Where is Your Bible?

Acknowledgements

Thank you to

- Sherma who keeps giving me ideas of topics, is a faithful sounding board about topics and so encouraging!
- Viv who is my computer techy person as well as friend and prayer warrior.
- Jodi who can quote scripture and knows where to find it!
- Lynette who challenged me to write about difficult subjects!
- Leanne for her words of encouragement and challenging me with new ideas to keep writing.
- Linda for her faithful reading, sense of humor and words of encouragement.
- Our Lord and Savior for the timeless words in the scripture that reach out to me in every aspect of my life.

"Karen has been given a beautiful gift from God in writing these devotionals. God is so good as He leads her, giving her His words to say to help, encourage, convict and to just come along side and just be silent in His presence. Keep up the good work. I sense a fourth book coming . . . "

Lynette Vanderhof

"Karen loops the heart of God into the weavings of the love of crocheting and knitting into the devotionals, *Prayer Shawl Ponderings*, *Prayer Shawl Reflections* and now *Prayer Shawl Encouragement*. She helps keep our eyes focused on the Master weaver, our Lord Jesus Christ. She reminds us that HE weaves all the circumstances of our life for His glory and for our good. Thank you Karen for your heart to serve the Lord through these devotionals and Prayer Shawl Ministries."

Vivian Ver Hoeven

I am so blessed to have connected with Karen through her Prayer Shawl Ministry and our ministry at our church. Our prayer shawl group has used Karen's books as devotionals for our meetings. We have enjoyed them so much and have good discussions after sharing them together each time. It is so wonderful to be able to use a devotional that is directly related to what we do, whether to be the giver of a shawl or as in some of our cases a recipient or both.

Thankful to call Karen, my Friend.

Mary Hulst

Karen's inspired stories are laced with scripture and give her readers applications for daily living. She gives the reader the ability to apply scripture to daily life through her inspirational stories.

Leanne Moen

Karen's devotionals are an inspirational and uplifting way to begin each day. One can find ways of serenity, hope, and peace through the readings. It is a blessing to have her God-filled insights on these pages.

Linda Vander Kamp

Praying it Forward

"Father, I want those You have given Me to be with me where I am and to see My glory, the glory You have given Me because You loved Me before the creation of the world" (John 17:24).

Paying it forward has become a popular thing. When ordering your food or drink, you pay for the order of the person behind you. What a nice surprise for that person to get out their money and find that their order has been paid for!

We can PRAY it forward with our prayer shawls. While we are making them, we don't always know who will receive it. So we pray for whatever the circumstance and the person to whom the shawl will be given.

In the garden of Gethsemane, Jesus prayed for what He knew was going to happen to Him in the next few days. One of His disciples would betray Him, another would deny he even knew Him (not once, but three times), He would have an unfair trial, be brutally beaten and hung to die on the cross, all for something He did not do.

Do you ever think of what Jesus was thinking for himself? He was willing to give His life, but would the human race even be willing to accept that He died for their sins. Did they deserve it? Would they appreciate what He was willing to do? Every person you see is someone Jesus thought enough of to die for, remember that in how you treat others.

We know He struggled with having to give His life. Luke 22:42 shows us Jesus' request of the Father, "Father, if you are willing, take this cup from me; yet not my will, but Yours be done." In verse 44, it tells us that His sweat was like drops of blood. It could possibly be hematidrosis, the actual mingling of blood and sweat as in cases of extreme anguish, strain or sensitivity.

When we are making our prayer shawls, we sometimes have thoughts of doubt about who will receive the shawl. Will they like the colors, the size or the stitch we made it with? Will they appreciate it or be embarrassed? So we pray it forward! Pray for the person to be receptive to the shawl and the prayers that it represents. Pray for the situation, for grace for that person as well as those around them. We need to step over our own insecurity about the shawl and let it be God's vessel to reach out to that person.

Aren't you glad that Jesus found us worthy to pay it forward for?

How Marvelous!

"But because of His great love for us, God, who is rich in mercy, made us alive with Christ even when we were dead in transgressions – it is by grace you have been saved" (Ephesians 2:4-5).

What a blessing to wake having my first thoughts be words to a song. Several times I have been awakened with the words, "He took my sin and my sorrow and made them His very own" ("I Stand Amazed" by Charles H Gabriel). All these struggles of daily life that I find so overwhelming, He took them and made them His own! Then He took them to Calvary and died alone.

The day-to-day life of going to work, all the politics, getting along with other people, making the customer happy are all part of me being God's hands in this world. Sometimes it is hard to believe that God is there in the workplace when things are chaotic. He is in all the politics of our country and world; He is there in our church struggles. God takes that sin and sorrow, makes it His own and forgives! When my attitude isn't what it should be, He is there with me. When life is good and cheerful, He is there!

Recently, I heard a message about difficult things in life. The pastor encouraged us to find out what God wanted us to learn in these situations. It is easy to grumble about the situation and pray that it changes. But do we think about praying for ways that we can learn and grow in the situation? God gave difficult things to His people in the Bible. Abraham was told to move his household to a country where he didn't know anybody and wasn't sure why he was there. But he obediently followed God's commands. God asked a very difficult thing of Jesus by sending Him to earth to live as a human being for 33 years, minister to people who didn't welcome Him, and die a cruel death. How marvelous that Jesus did that for us!

The last verse of "I Stand Amazed" is "When with the ransomed in glory His face I at last shall see, 'Twill be my joy through the ages to sing of His love for me." Because of Jesus dying on the cross, we have Heaven to anticipate!

Giving Thanks

"Be joyful always; pray continually; give thanks in all circumstance, for this is God's will for you in Christ Jesus" (I Thessalonians 5:16-18).

What if you woke up TODAY with only the things that you THANKED GOD for yesterday? Are you able to get your mind around that? All those things we take for granted that will be there tomorrow, whether we thank God for them or not. We not only have clean water, we have it coming from a faucet in several sinks in our house, and it is hot and cold as we need it. Many people in the world have to walk for several miles to get water that isn't clean and has bacteria in it which can cause sickness. They carry it home on their heads or a container in each hand. Think about how much water we use in a day for cooking, cleaning, washing clothes, bathing and drinking. We take it for granted that we can take a shower at least once a day. Living in some countries, that would all have to be carried in.

We come and go about our daily life taking it for granted that we have a home, a vehicle that will take us where we want to go, and stores well supplied with everything we could possibly want or need. We have our health and grumble when we don't feel well, "I don't have time for this."

I Thessalonians 5:16-18 tells us, "Be joyful always; pray continually; give thanks in all circumstances, for this is God's will for you in Christ Jesus." Christians are differentiated from the natural man. Because of what God has done, they are continually thankful whatever the circumstance. That isn't always easy to

10

do! Life happens and we are treated unfairly, the workplace is not a pleasant place to be, family members are difficult to get along with and we are to be thankful!

There is a song that says, "I've a roof up above me, a good place to sleep, food on the table and shoes on my feet. Thank you, Lord, for your blessings on me." (Easter) This was written by a man who lived in a shack in a junkyard, where he could see the stars through his roof. How often do we thank God for what we consider the basics of life? A bed, roof over our heads, food, shoes on our feet, even the very air we breathe!

While we are praying over the shawl we are making, we need to remember to give thanks as well as all the requests we are praying. Thank God for the person who will receive the shawl. We may not know who that person is, but God sure knows. Thank God for being able to knit or crochet and have the ability to buy the yarn and make the shawl. You have a warm place to be, a comfortable chair to sit in, a light over your head, and God's peace in your heart. May the shawl you are making be a beacon in the home where it goes, telling the recipient and family of all those who are bringing their name before the throne of Grace.

Are you grumbling because roses have thorns or are you being thankful that thorns have roses?

Jonah Days

"Your attitude should be the same as that of Christ Jesus" (Philippians 2:5).

Do you ever have Jonah days? You know the days when nothing is right. It seems you started your day be getting out of the wrong side of the bed. The sun isn't shining, the sun is shining too bright, clouds, not enough clouds, she said, he said, nothing is right. The hardest part of those days is that we create them ourselves most of the time.

Once we start looking at the "wrong" side of things, we can't see anything else. We blame others and things for how we feel. A favorite one to blame for women is hormones. Hormones do play a part, but probably not as big of a part for which we give them credit. It's like giving the devil credit for everything that happens. Don't let him have too much credit! We aren't very lovable on those days.

God called Jonah to go to Nineveh to preach to the people. Jonah didn't want to, so he hopped a ship going 2,800 miles exactly the opposite direction. How often don't we run from what God wants us to do? A storm came and threatened to sink the ship. By casting lots, Jonah knew he was being punished. He fessed up to the sailors, and told them to throw him overboard. They did and the sea calmed. From this, the sailors believed in God. A whale swallowed Jonah and he spent three days in its belly. He called out to God. The whale upchucked him on the beach and God gave Jonah a second chance to go to Nineveh. Jonah took the opportunity and went to Ninevah. Many people in

Nineveh humbled themselves before God and He was gracious to them and didn't destroy the city.

Then Jonah had a melt down! He was angry at God for having compassion on an enemy of Israel. He wanted God's goodness to be shown only to Israelites, not to Gentiles. Jonah goes and sits under his shelter feeling sorry for himself. God sends a vine to grow and give him shade. God then allows the heat to kill the vine. Jonah wants to die and he's angry about the vine dying. God chats with him. "You didn't make the vine grow and yet you are angry about it dying. Nineveh has more than one hundred and twenty thousand people who are so immature they don't know their right hand from their left. Should I not be concerned about all those people?" (Jonah 4:10-11) God had the last word and left Jonah to adjust his attitude.

How often don't we run from what God wants us to do? It isn't always literally, although that might be the case. I'm talking about the times we ignore what we're supposed to do. That's a form of running from God.

Even God wasn't doing the right things to suit Jonah. It seems Jonah would have a hard time living with himself let alone anyone else. I wonder if he had a hormone problem? Instead of premenstrual syndrome (PMS), he had prophet mood swings (PMS)! Are we like that? Always negative thoughts. The glass is always half empty.

The end of the book of Jonah does not give us a happy ending. It is the only book of the Bible that ends with a question. Jonah was still angry. Verse 9 of chapter 4 says, "I am angry enough to die." Compare that to Job who repented in dust and ashes and then praised God. The book of Job ends with, "And so he died, old and full of years."

We can choose to make life bitter or better. Have your Jonah days, but then get over them! Move on with David in Psalm 42:5,

"Why are you downcast, O my soul? Why so disturbed within me? Put your hope in God, for I will yet praise Him, my Savior and my God." Christians are to have the attitude of Christ in spite of all that is unique and radically different about the person and work of Christ. Christians are to have His attitude of self-sacrificing humility and love for others.

Ironically, Jonah was the most successful prophet because according to 4:11, one hundred and twenty thousand people were saved. God can work wonders with us, even with our Jonah attitudes!

Survive or Thrive

"Come to me, all you who are weary and burdened, and I will give you rest. Take my yoke upon you and learn from me, for I am gentle and humble in heart and you will find rest for your souls. For my yoke is easy and my burden is light" (Matthew 11:29-30).

Are you plodding through life, just getting one foot ahead of the other, surviving one day at a time? Life is heavy. It may be the work situation you are in, grieving the loss of a loved one, health issues, life changes that were not your choice, or concerns of family relationships are some of the things that pull us down emotionally. Concerns for our country, its morals, politics and the lack of true statesmen who are leading our country for the country's good and not their own interests are age old concerns. We become so burdened that we find surviving is the only way to keep going.

Psalm 43 shows us these feelings are not new in our generation. In verse 1 of the King James Version, it uses the word "judge" and the NIV uses "vindicate me, O God, and plead my cause against an ungodly nation." Webster's dictionary tells us that to vindicate is to clear someone of blame or suspicion, show or prove to be right. To judge is to form an opinion about someone or something after careful thought, to regard someone as either good or bad. The psalmist is asking God to judge or vindicate him against an ungodly nation and wicked men. He also feels like God has rejected him. That would certainly put you in survival mode!

The psalmist knew Who to go to with his barely surviving attitude. He sought God and asked for His light and truth. He wanted to thrive in this sinful world and he knew God would be the source for that attitude. In verse 4, he chooses to go to the altar of God "my joy and my delight." Matthew 11:29-30 gives us reassurance that God is willing to take that burden and carry it for us. Those restful words that assure and bring us to the last verse of Psalm 43, "Why are you downcast, O my soul? Why so disturbed within me? Put your hope in God, for I will yet praise Him, my Savior and my God." The Psalmist must have struggled with this, because Psalm 42 also talks about being overwhelmed with life, but it ends with these same words. Do you think God wants us to hear those words? The Message tells us in Romans 8:15, "This resurrection life you received from God is not a timid, grave-tending life. It's adventurously expectant, greeting God with a childlike 'What's next, Papa?'"

The acronym of JOY is Jesus first, others second, and yourself last. If we live this, we will not have time to dwell on our problems or sometimes create a problem where none exist.

While you are knitting or crocheting your prayer shawls, make the choice to thrive in this world. Our prayer shawls can be the altar where we lay down the survival mode and choose to thrive by reaching out to others in this hurting world.

Letting Go

Our prayer shawl group sent a box of shawls to Washington, Illinois, when they had a tornado go through their town in 2014. They in turn shared them with the people in Arkansas when they had a tornado go through their town on April 27, 2014. We received this note from one of the recipients of some shawls.

"In a roundabout way, I received a prayer shawl you knitted and I just want to say a huge thank you. God knew I needed it.

On April 27 this year, my family of 8 were home when a tornado completely destroyed our house, cars and all. We were all safe, with our pets, too, in our bedroom closet, which thankfully was built as a safe room. The experience and the aftermath have been difficult although God is good and gracious.

This summer we received a package from Washington, Illinois, with some extra gifts from the tornado they had a year ago. Inside was the shawl you made and a few others from your church group. I have slept with mine ever since. When I wake in the night, it reminds me to pray. It has brought so much comfort to me.

My children also love the ones they received - It means so much to have the homemade items since we lost so many. Thank you again to you and your group for loving and praying for us! God bless you!"

17

We never know where our shawls will end up. When we are making them, we pray for the recipient and their situation. We make the gift and then give it with no physical strings attached. Let go and let God. Our shawls may end up wrapped around shoulders of a Christian and be a source of comfort to them knowing other Christians are praying for them. They can reach out to someone who knows about Christianity, but has been hurt by someone in the church or the church itself. They need reassurance that someone is praying for them. A shawl can reach out to a total unbeliever and pull them toward a believer or reach out to the church that is printed on the card that is attached to the prayer shawl. A shawl can be ministering when laying on a table at a garage sale. The prayers don't have an expiration date or are meant for just one person. Those prayers can touch everyone who handles that prayer shawl. Don't underestimate the power of prayer and of our great God!

Praying Victoriously

Prayer request time in a group of people is a wonderful sharing time. It is a time when we can share our praise, concerns and interact with fellow Christians. God loves it when we come to Him for the things we need and to become the person He wants us to be. "We have to be careful that we shouldn't spend more time talking about our requests than we do praying for them," is what Stormie O'Martian tells us in her book, The Power of the Praying Woman. Before you speak up to make a prayer request, consider carefully the fine line of gossip and information. We humans don't need to know all the details about a situation, all that is needed is the person's first name and a brief sentence of their concerns. God knows the details, we just need to give Him the request, not tell Him how we want it fixed. Matthew 6:7-8 (NLT) tells us, "When you pray, don't babble on and on as people of other religions do. They think their prayers are answered merely by repeating their words again and again. Don't be like them, for your Father knows exactly what you need even before you ask Him!" The passage goes on to give us the perfect prayer, the Lord's Prayer.

After we have voiced our prayer requests, consider a "blanket" prayer that states, "Lord, you have heard these requests and we bring them before Your throne." Then proceed with praising Him, and thanking Him for salvation. The acronym ACTS is a great way to structure our prayers.

- Adoration - "Praise be to God!" Psalms 68:35. Tell God how much you appreciate Him. Express your love for Him. Praise His power and majesty. You should never run out of praise. "How awesome are your deeds!" Psalms 66:3. If adoration is difficult, pray one of the psalms!

- Confession – "If we confess our sins, He is faithful and just, and will forgive us our sins and purify us from all unrighteousness" I John 1:9. Tell Him where you have fallen short. Thank Him for the forgiveness we have in Christ, and ask for help and strength to turn away from future temptations.

- Thanksgiving – "Glorify Him with thanksgiving" Psalms 69:30. Thank God for His love, faithfulness, patience and a million other things. Thank Him for what He is doing in your life. Thank Jesus for dying on the cross for you, the Holy Spirit for dwelling in you and never leaving. Thank Him for being your conscience, your counselor and that "still small voice."

- Supplication – "Make your requests known to God" Philippians 4:6. Tell God what you want, nothing is too big or too small for our God.

While we are working on our prayer shawls, it is easy to fall into a continuous supplication mode. Consider saying one of the many names for God with each stitch you make. Praise Him, thank Him! Psalm 34:1 tells us, "I will extol the Lord at all times; His praise will always be on my lips."

The only prayer God cannot answer is the one that has never been prayed.

Rest in Peace

"And we urge you, brothers, warn those who are idle, encourage the timid, help the weak" (I Thessalonians 5:14).

An elderly lady was part of a prayer shawl group and was busy praying and knitting a shawl. God took her home to heaven while she was knitting. Think of it! She was talking to her Savior and in the next instant she was in His presence. What a gift! Her family buried her with the knitting needles and the shawl. What comfort for her family that they knew where she was going! I Thessalonians 4:10 tells us, "He died for us so that, whether we are awake or asleep, we may live together with Him."

This lady was certainly living I Thessalonians 4:11-12, "and to make it your ambition to lead a quiet life; You should mind your own business and work with your hands, just as we told you, so that your daily life may win the respect of outsiders and so that you will not be dependent on anybody." Are you willing to have Jesus sit beside you in all your activities? The books you read, movies you watch, or where you spend your social time. A gal in our Prayer Shawl group has made the commitment to not read any books that she would be ashamed to have Jesus read with her.

The Thessalonian people were so sure that Jesus' second coming was soon that they had given up their jobs to prepare for it. Only God knows when Jesus will come again, not even Jesus or the Holy Spirit are aware of the day or the hour. Until Jesus comes or He takes us home, we are to keep busy doing the work

God gives to us. We "yarnies" would want to keep a supply of yarn on hand and keep at the knitting and crocheting.

The epitaph on Ruth Graham's tombstone says, "End of construction, thank you for your patience." In this life, we are all under continuous construction. A construction zone is a busy, working, growing zone. We must be patient with each other as the construction process continues. Make good use of the time He gives to each of us. We never know the day or the hour that Jesus may come or He may call us home to Him.

The Courage of Your Convictions

Dr. Ted Fazier was the director of the North American Baptist Seminary Choir for many years. I sang in that choir for several years. He wanted us to get on that first note of a song or line "with all the courage of your convictions." He wanted us there in full voice, not just easing into it. Of course, he preferred for us to be on the correct note! We sang "The Messiah" every Christmas and the Hallelujah chorus just needs all the courage of your convictions on that first note of Hallelujah!

Are we in God's Word with all the courage of our convictions? Are we willing to talk to others about our salvation with conviction? We have a friend who will walk up to people on the street and ask them if they know where they will spend eternity. How many of us are willing to stand up for our faith like that? We can talk about everything else under the sun, but not about our salvation. Is it because we are afraid of being "politically incorrect," or offending people with our beliefs? Jesus is very clear in Matthew 10:32-33, "Whoever acknowledges me before men, I will also acknowledge him before My Father in heaven. But whoever disowns me before men, I will disown him before My Father in heaven."

In the Old Testament, after God had given Israel the Ten Commandments, He urged them, "These commandments that I give you today are to be upon your hearts. Impress them on your children. Talk about them when you sit at home and when you walk along the road, when you lie down and when you get up. Tie them as symbols on your hands and bind them on your foreheads. Write them on the doorframes of your houses and on

23

your gates" (Deuteronomy 6:6-9). Are we willing to talk about our wonderful salvation in our day-to-day life? Are we doing it with the courage of our convictions? This thought is reemphasized in I Peter 3:15, "But in your hearts set apart Christ as Lord. Always be prepared to give an answer to everyone who asks you to give the reason for the hope that you have. But do this with gentleness and respect." We are being asked to make an inner commitment to Christ so we are not speechless when called on to defend our faith.

The Prayer Shawl ministry is a wonderful way of opening up conversations about our faith. When talking about the ministry, it has to be explained that we pray while we make the shawl, for the person who will receive the shawl as well as those around that person and their situation. Pray with the courage of your conviction! God wants to hear those words from your lips and heart!

Forgetting What is Behind

"… forgetting what is behind and straining toward what is ahead" (Philippians 3:13).

We each have the "tapes" playing in our heads of things that have been said or done in the past that we just can't put away. Some people have "card files" to pull up past indiscretions. It may be our mother's voice reminding us or telling us what to do or not do. If our parents were critical, moralizing or overprotective, we will carry the results of those attitudes with us. We also carry the positive criticism of our parents. These black tapes also produce negative labels, which we apply to ourselves. Spending time alone when we get to thinking about things from the past can allow for those memories to flash back. We can push those thoughts back as hard as we can, but until we replace them with positive thoughts, there will be room for them to "live" there.

Interestingly, males respond to criticism with anger and ignore feedback. Females tend to create an inner list, keeping score of everything they did wrong. When being criticized, listen carefully, and pick out the positive parts for golden nuggets that can help you. We must not accept the irrational assumption that something is wrong with us. Constructive criticism is actually a form of encouragement.

First John 1:9 assures us, "If we confess our sins, He is faithful and just and will forgive us our sins and purify us from all unrighteousness." Not all the tapes playing in our heads are sin, but for whatever reason, Satan doesn't want us to forget those things. God is asking us to confess our sins to Him and then let it go.

Philippians 3:14 goes on with, "I press on toward the goal to win the prize for which God has called me heavenward in Christ Jesus." Our ultimate goal is not found in this life, but in everlasting glory in heaven.

As we spend time praying while we knit and crochet, fill that time with praising and honoring God, thanking Him for the opportunity and ability to make a shawl, and praying for the person who receives it and their situation. We need to crowd out those negative thoughts and replace them with positive thoughts.

Peace

"And the peace of God, which transcends all understanding, will guard your hearts and your minds in Christ Jesus" (Philippians 4:7).

In 2013, our prayer shawl group sent a box of shawls to a church near Sandy Hook Elementary school where many children and teachers were shot by a gunman. They distributed over 1,500 shawls to grieving friends, bus drivers, neighbors who were troubled, fire fighters, etc. The mother of a girl that was killed on December 14 said that as soon as she put the shawl on, she felt peace.

In the chaos after that shooting, when everyone around was anxious and concerned, to be given a shawl that brings peace to your heart had to be a blessing from God. This was not just a mental state, but an inner tranquility based on peace with God. It's a peaceful state of one who knows their sins are forgiven. We are able to cast all our cares on God and He gives us peace. We can leave it in His hands; He is in control of it all!

Karen's brother-in-law recently had his second kidney removed because of cancer. He is on dialysis for the rest of his life. He is not eligible for a kidney transplant until two years after the surgery and then he will be 75 years old. Karen made a shawl for him. He had it over his arms at dialysis and all the prayers and love that went into it made a huge difference to him. He usually would sleep when he got home from dialysis, but this day he came home and was hungry. "All your love and prayers entered his body and he has been so good! We both thank you

27

for the love of God that entered Warren's body through yours!" his wife told Karen. The prayer shawl was a tangible reminder for him of all the people praying for him. He was physically too spent to think of those who are praying for him.

God's love and care stands "guard" around those who are in Christ Jesus and extends to the core of their beings and to their deepest intentions. It is hard to comprehend the depth of God's love and care. Ephesians 3:18 says, "(You) may have power together with all the saints, to grasp how wide and long and high and deep is the love of Christ." Only God knows the infiniteness of His love. We just rest peacefully in those loving arms that hold us. God is using us to make the prayer shawls and pray over them to bless those who need to be upheld and give them His peace.

What is Your Gift?

"Then they opened their treasures and presented Him with gifts of gold and of incense and of myrrh" (Matthew 2:11).

Gifts can come in many sizes and shapes and sometimes it isn't a "thing" at all. It can be your gift of time. The shepherds gave Jesus the gift of their time by coming out of the fields and going to visit the new baby, praising Him. Then they spread the word that Jesus had been born.

The Magi brought their gifts of gold, incense and myrrh as well their gift of not telling King Herod the location of the baby Jesus. It is said that gold represents virtue, incense represents prayer, and myrrh represents suffering. The oil of myrrh was used in beauty treatments and sometimes mixed with wine and drunk to relieve pain. As a gift fit for a king, myrrh was brought to Jesus after His birth and applied to His body after His death.

The Magi had been warned in a dream not to return to Herod after they found Jesus, so they returned home a different way. King Herod, known for his temper, became very angry when he found out what the magi had done. So he had all the little boys under two years old that lived in Bethlehem killed. Meanwhile, Mary and Joseph slipped out of town with their new baby. So the gift of the Magi of not telling Herod of their finding Him saved Jesus' life.

What gift do we have for Jesus? We can give Him the gift of our time to make prayer shawls and bring them to a hurting person. Part of our gift is the cost of yarn, but the greater gift is the prayers we pray for the person who receives the shawl. Our gift of encouraging words is appreciated, but sometimes the gift of just "being there" brings great comfort. Sometimes words are overrated!

Our willingness to be God's hands in making prayer shawls is also a gift. Psalm 51:10 tells us, "Create in me a pure heart, O God, and renew a steadfast spirit within me." We are asking for a pure heart, a steadfast spirit of faithfulness, and a willing spirit of service. We underestimate our gift of being able to knit or crochet, something many people are not able to do, but we need a willing spirit to go with our talent.

Feeding on His Word

"I have hidden Your word in my heart that I might not sin against You" (Psalm 119:11).

When we are looking at new or different knit or crochet patterns, we glance over it quickly to see how involved and complicated it is. Sometimes we want easy and straightforward, and other times, we are looking for a challenge. When we sit down to actually work the pattern, we read it step by step and do the directions, sometimes word by word. We make a row, check to see how it looks, tear it out and do it again until we get the right look. Pictures of the stitches and finished item can be very helpful.

We can read God's Word quickly, following the guidelines of a "through the Bible in a year" process. We are reading several chapters in a day and that is a good way to be able to read the whole Bible. But there are times that we need to feed on God's Word, taking one verse or even part of a verse at a time.

We need to take the time to read scripture slowly and carefully, listening for what the Spirit is saying. We can read a verse today and depending on the situation we are in or the mood we are in, that verse can reach out to us in one way. Later, we can read that same verse over again and find new truths and different meaning.

God, in His infinite wisdom, had the Bible written to meet needs in all situations, personalities, age groups and even our human moods. God knew how we humans would need reassurance from Him for every situation in life.

Feeding on God's Word is His way of talking to us. We so quickly want to bring our requests and "suggestions" to God, but we need to take time to feed on His Word and to listen for Him to speak to us. We need to spend time just being quiet before the Lord.

God longs for us to take time to spend with Him. The words to the song "Take Time to be Holy" say it so well. "Take time to be holy, speak oft with thy Lord. Abide in Him always, and feed on His Word. Make friends of God's children, Help those who are weak, Forgetting in nothing His blessing to seek," (George C. Stebbins, 1846-1847). We carefully nurture relationships with our human friends, why wouldn't we do it with our best Friend? The efforts we put into the relationship with Jesus while we are on earth will prepare us for eternity when we see our Best Friend face to face.

Whiter than Snow

"Cleanse me with hyssop and I will be clean; wash me, and I will be whiter than snow" (Psalm 51:7).

So have you pulled out that stove and refrigerator lately and cleaned up the sticky (I didn't say stinky!) dust bunnies that have accumulated there? Cleaning the kitchen can be so rewarding when it is all shiny clean. Are all the corners and edges gleaming clean? Can we ever have a spotless kitchen? You cook one meal and it quickly becomes dirty again. Then there is our favorite craft bag that has all kinds of treasures at the bottom. Small balls of yarn, buttons from who knows where, safety pins, candy wrappers (oops-who put that in there?) underneath our current project of yarn. Is anything ever really clean?

Watching the snow fall softly we see how white, clean and pure it is. Then it lays on the ground for a short time and there is sand, dirt, animals walking over it, people walk and drive over it, and the white, cleanness soon dims. Isaiah 1:18 tells us, "Come now, let us reason together, says the Lord. Though your sins are like scarlet, they shall be a white as snow; thought they are red as crimson, they shall be like wool." The scarlet and red is the dirt and sin in our life, then comes the white snow to make us clean. Psalm 51:7 asks God to "Cleanse me with hyssop and I will be clean; wash me, and I will be whiter than snow."

We make our prayer shawls from new yarn that was bought in the store. But is the yarn really clean? As we work on it, the oils from our hands get on the yarn, if there is a pet in the house, the hair gets on the yarn, or our own hair gets on the yarn. Once again, can anything be really clean?

Cleanse me can literally be interpreted as "un-sin" me. Like a filthy garment, we need washing, and if God washes us, we will be so pure that there is no figurative word that can describe us. Part of our prayer while we are knitting or crocheting should be "wash me and I will be whiter than snow."

Sing to the Lord

"Sing to the Lord, praise His name; proclaim His salvation day after day" (Psalm 96:2).

Dr. Ted Fazier, who directed the North American Baptist Seminary Choir for many years, would start rehearsals with the choir singing one of the old hymns from the hymnal. Then he would use the words of the song as the devotional. When we are singing we get so focused on the tune, what our part is, and how it sounds that we ignore the beauty and spiritual truths of the words to the songs.

Music and the choice of songs is a sensitive subject in churches. The congregations are made up of people with diversity in age, interests and intelligence, so the music should be diverse enough for each person to appreciate a song that feeds them spiritually. The music is there to set the tone and prepare our hearts for the message that is going to be given. It is difficult when there are new songs and we don't have music to follow. Find your inspiration in reading the words and focus on the meaning of the words. Colossians 3:16 tells us, "Let the word of Christ dwell in you richly as you teach and admonish one another with all wisdom, and as you sing psalms, hymns and spiritual songs with gratitude in your hearts to God."

If you have been following along in the previous two books of devotions that I have written, you notice that music is a big part of my life and my worship. It makes me grumpy when there are no songs sung in a service that I can sing along to because I don't know any of them. I have to work on my attitude, appreciate the words that are being sung by others and get my heart in a worshipful attitude.

There are crochet and knit patterns that make us grumpy, because we don't understand the pattern and it just doesn't want to be made. It is important to have a worshipful attitude about everything in life. Don't miss the opportunity to sing to the Lord in all aspects of your life. While we are making shawls we can be singing His praises, listening to music that praises Him and making that a part of our prayers.

In this ever-changing world of music, patterns and technology, isn't it wonderful to know that "Jesus Christ is the same yesterday and today and forever" (Hebrews 13:8).

Kind Words

"Set a guard over my mouth, O Lord; keep watch over the door of my lips" (Psalm 141:3).

One of my mom's favorite sayings to her kids was, "If you can't say anything nice, don't say anything at all." When I am all geared up with a sharp retort to someone and suddenly that thought comes to mind, there is a big quiet!

We are so quick to point out what we consider to be weaknesses in family, friends or work colleagues. We choose to focus on their mistakes rather than their successes. Paul tells us in James 3:5, "Likewise the tongue is a small part of the body, but it makes great boasts." The tongue is so difficult to control, anyone who controls it perfectly, gains control of himself in all other areas of life as well.

When making prayer shawls, I like to make granny squares of many different colors and then crochet them together with black yarn. One lady commented that she liked the granny squares, but "wasn't crazy about the black!" Of the many positive, thankful comments we receive about prayer shawls, that comment seems to stay with me.

One way of checking ourselves is before we say something, consider if it is helping or hindering the person to whom we will say it. We don't want to become a stumbling block for someone who is struggling to find Jesus' way in this world.

When asking a silversmith how he knew when the silver was at the correct heat and melted enough, he said when he saw himself in the melted silver, then he knew it was just right. Can Jesus see Himself in you and in the words you say? The melting process can be painful, but it is also very rewarding.

Ecclesiastes 5:2 tells us, "Do not be quick with your mouth, do not be hasty in your heart to utter anything before God. God is in heaven and you are on earth so let your words be few." He reminds us to think about what we say. When we speak quickly we tend to say rash things. The verse goes on with, "God is in heaven and you are on earth, so let your words be few." Sometimes less words or no words are a better choice. There is a song that talks about our actions of love that speak so loudly and then, if that fails, use words.

Words can be vinegar or honey; you collect more friends with honey. Honor God with your words and may they be seasoned with honey!

Calling on Him

"The Lord is near to all who call on Him, to all who call on Him in truth" (Psalm 145:18).

If you call me at home on the telephone, you may have to run the gauntlet of talking to my husband. If you ask if I am available, he will tell you I am married. If you ask if I am around, he will tell you I am a square today. If you ask if I am there, he will say yes and then leave a long pause, then ask if you want to talk to me.

When we "call" God, we don't need to answer any of those questions and we don't need to go through anyone else to get to Him. We don't have to wait in line; He is available any time of day or night. We have direct access to God. Hebrews 10:22 (NLT) tells us, "Let us go right into the presence of God with sincere hearts fully trusting Him."

Hebrews 4:16 encourages us to, "Let us then approach the throne of grace with confidence so that we may receive mercy and find grace to help us in our time of need." Jesus has experienced our human temptation, and He stands ready to give immediate and sympathetic help when we are struggling. He encourages us to pray with confidence. We don't always get our desired answer, but He still wants us to bring our cares and concerns to Him.

His answer may be yes, no or wait. The cartoonist Bryan Crane who writes Pickles has Nelson, the grandson, asking his grandfather if he prays before he goes to bed. Grandfather answers, "You bet! I heard a fella say that there are just two reasons to pray ... one is to say "help me" and the other is to say "thank you." Nelson answers, "How about just to say 'Hi'"? Spending time in God's waiting room stretches our patience, but it also builds character. Through this all, we know that God is near and upholding us in our situation. That doesn't always sink into our finite minds as we are struggling through a difficult time. We all experience "dry" times in our life. Life becomes difficult with loss of family and friends to death, stressful work situations, illness for yourself and loved ones and difficult home situations. God didn't move, He is there waiting and holding you.

The Joy of Your Salvation

"Restore to me the joy of Your salvation and grant me a willing spirit, to sustain me" (Psalm 51:12).

Many times, we let life weigh us down and forget about the wonder of our salvation. The Bible is full of verses that tell us to rejoice, to joy in what God has done for us. So often we choose to be over humble, to carry on that we are not good enough. People have even chosen not to accept God's salvation or join a church until they are good enough. Then we are back to doing good works trying to earn our salvation. Salvation is a free gift from God. We cannot earn it.

Philippians 4:4 tells us, "Be full of joy always because you belong to the Lord. Again I say, be full of joy!" (NLT) The apostle Paul felt it was so important, he said it twice, "Be full of joy!" We will not always be in a joyful mood. There will be hard times when God is carrying us through. We will always know that we have the peace of our salvation in our hearts. Isaiah 35:10 and Isaiah 51:11 repeat the exact verse, "And the ransomed of the Lord will return. They will enter Zion with singing; everlasting joy will crown their heads. Gladness and joy will overtake them, and sorrow and sighing will flee away." The Israelites were being pursued by gladness and joy as they returned from Babylon. God wants us to be pursued by joy and gladness throughout our lives. While we are experiencing and after a dark time in our life, we will experience God's gladness, joy and peace.

Our prayer shawls are there to remind people of others who are praying for them as well as reminding them of the joy of their salvation. When we are going through difficult times, it feels like we are so alone. First, God is there all along and second, we have fellow believers who are praying and coming alongside of us. First John 4:11-12 says, "Dear friends, since God so loved us, we also ought to love one another. No one has ever seen God; but if we love one another, God lives in us and His love is made complete in us."

I am using a lot of Bible passages in this devotion, but I so want you to understand that the joy of our salvation is God's choice and a free gift for us.

Dedicated

"Always work enthusiastically for the Lord, for you know that nothing you do for the Lord is ever useless" (I Corinthians 15:58 NLT).

We "yarnies" are quite dedicated to our craft projects. Wanda enjoys crocheting while riding with her husband on their motorcycle. Ann enjoys knitting while riding her exercise bike. Lila is knitting or crocheting any time she is riding along with someone in the car. When I speak at the Days of Encouragement that have been held, I enjoy seeing the ladies knitting and crocheting while I speak. I know how well they can multitask!

God wants us to enjoy what we are doing for work or pleasure. In Matthew 25, Jesus is teaching the Parable of the Talents. The term talent was first used for a unit of weight, then for a unit of currency. The present day use of "talent" indicating an ability or gift is taken from this parable. The two servants who wisely invested the talents given to them were rewarded with the words from verses 21 and 23, "Well done, good and faithful servant! You have been faithful with a few things; I will put you in charge of many things. Come and share your Master's happiness!"

The talent of knitting and crocheting is a blessing from God. We aren't aware of how many people don't have any idea how to do either one. We are blessed that we can use this talent in making prayer shawls for the hurting people in our world. First Peter 4:10 tells us, "Each one should use whatever gift he has received to serve others, faithfully administering God's grace in its various forms."

Because Jesus came to earth, suffered, died and was resurrected, we know that serving Him is not empty, useless activity. "Your labor in the Lord is not vain (useless)" (1 Corinthians 15:58 NIV). Our efforts of knitting, crocheting and being a part of the Prayer Shawl ministry is all done for the greater cause of Jesus Christ.

Hell is for Real

"Where their worm (maggot) dieth not, and the fire is not quenched" (Mark 9:48).

In our world today, there is a general feeling of denial that there is a hell. The Bible is very graphic about what hell will be like. First, you will lose all the pleasures and enjoyment that you knew here on earth. Matthew 8:12 describes hell as follows: "But the subjects of the kingdom will be thrown outside, into the darkness, where there will be weeping and gnashing of teeth." Being separated from God is an emotional and physical punishment. Charles Spurgeon tells us, "The Lord Jesus Christ spoke more about hell than about Heaven, and He always described hell in terms of fire and physical torment. "Where their worm dieth not, and the fire is not quenched" (Mark 9:44, 46, 48). Hell is described as "fire" (Mt. 5:22; 18:9), "everlasting fire" (Mt. 18:8; 25:41), "fire unquenchable" (Luke 3:17), "this flame" (Lk. 16:24), "furnace of fire" (Mt." 13:42, 50), "eternal fire" (Jude 7), and "fire and brimstone" (Rev. 14:10; 20:10; 21:8)." The second thing to remember about hell is that you will be eternally cut off from heaven and all who go there. Friends, family, loved ones and mostly, our Lord Jesus - we will be eternally separated from them. There is no sun or moon there.

People may joke about going to hell, but do they realize what they are considering? It is a place of emotional and physical torment, separated from God and there are no doors to exit the place. You are there to stay for eternity. John Wesley tells us, "There is no grandeur in the infernal regions; there is nothing beautiful in those dark abodes; no light but that of livid flames.

And nothing new, but one unvaried scene of horror upon horror! There is no music but that of groaning and shrieks; of weeping, wailing, and gnashing of teeth; of curses and blasphemies against God, or cutting reproaches of one another. Nor is there anything to gratify the sense of honour: No; they are the heirs of shame and everlasting contempt."

If we choose not to accept Jesus as our Lord and Savior, He will say to us, "Depart from Me, you who are cursed, into the eternal fire prepared for the devil and his angels" (Matthew 26:41).

We, as Christians, have the great comfort that God has conquered the grave and hell when He came to earth and died on the cross for our sins. Revelation 1:18 tells us, "I am the Living One; I was dead, and behold I am alive for ever and ever! And I hold the keys of death and Hades." God has absolute control over death and hell. We can rejoice with Paul in I Corinthians 15: 55, "Where, O death, is your victory? Where, O death, is your sting?"

While we are praying as we make our shawls, pray for the spiritual salvation of the recipient of your shawl. We are very aware of their hurting physically, emotionally, and spiritually while here on earth and we are praying for that. We need to also be praying for their life in eternity as well.

There are many different opinions about if there is a hell, if there is fire, and how often Jesus spoke about hell versus heaven. Above is listed some of the scriptures that verify there is indeed a hell and it is something to fear. Run to the cross! Accept Jesus as your personal Savior and Lord for this life and for eternity. Pray for those who have not accepted Him. God yearns to have everyone accept Him as their Lord and to surround them with His love.

Great is Thy Faithfulness

"They are new every morning; great is Your faithfulness" (Lamentation 3:23).

The Lord's faithfulness is beyond measure. Every morning, again and again, God is faithful. The author of Lamentations 3:1-18, who could be Jeremiah or an anonymous mourner, speaks not only for himself, but also for the suffering community of which he is a part. Then in verse 21, he changes his tone and he expounds on God's goodness and faithfulness. Our lives are so much like that. We need to go through hard times before we can really appreciate God's faithfulness.

Verse 40 gives us a plan for how to deal with difficulties in life, "Let us examine our ways and test them, and let us return to the Lord." We come around full circle - we stray from God, He allows difficult times and we return to Him for comfort and reassurance. We are not so different from the Old Testament children of Israel!

Lamentations 3:32-33 goes on to tell us, "Though He brings grief, He will show compassion, so great is His unfailing love. For He does not willingly bring affliction or grief to the children of man." The same God who judges also restores. Faithfulness and unfailing love are often used together to sum up God's promised mercies toward His people.

The song, "Great Is Thy Faithfulness" by William M. Runyan is a devotional unto itself.

Great is Thy faithfulness, O God my Father,
There is no shadow of turning with Thee;
Thou changest not, Thy compassions, they fail not;
As Thou hast been Thou forever wilt be.

Summer and winter and springtime and harvest,
Sun, moon and stars in their courses above
Join with all nature in manifold witness
To Thy great faithfulness, mercy and love.

Pardon for sin and a peace that endureth,
Thine own dear presence to cheer and to guide,
Strength for today and bright hope for tomorrow,
Blessings all mine, with ten thousand beside!

Chorus:
Great is Thy faithfulness! Great is Thy faithfulness!
Morning by morning new mercies I see;
All I have needed Thy hand hath provided,
Great is Thy faithfulness, Lord, unto me!

It is overwhelming to think of God's faithfulness to ME! How
unchanging He is!

Eyes

"The Lord turned and looked straight at Peter" (Luke 22:61).

Can you imagine making direct eye contact with Jesus? In this scripture, Jesus is looking at Peter after he had denied knowing Jesus not once, but three times. What did Peter see in Jesus' eyes? Was it a look of judgment, sadness or love?

When we arrive in heaven and Jesus is there waiting for us, our eyes will meet His. Will His eyes be brown or blue? I anticipate brown eyes that are soft with a look of love looking at me and welcoming me into His arms. Each of us can use our own imagination for what that will be like. Looking into someone's eyes is like reading body language, it speaks volumes! It is said that eyes are the window of the soul.

Can you imagine knitting or crocheting without your eyesight? As we age, we find it harder to work with dark colors, need better lighting, and do it for shorter periods of time because our eyes get tired as well as our shoulders, arms and hands. Keeping our eyes on the road while we drive or on our knitting/crocheting is important.

Some people can smile with their lips, but the smile never reaches their eyes. Other people can speak volumes with their eyes without ever saying a word. Jesus tells us in Matthew 6:22-23, "The eye is the lamp of the body. If your eyes are good, your whole body will be full of light. But if your eyes are bad, your whole body will be full of darkness. If then the light within you is darkness, how great is that darkness!"

This brings to mind the song we sang in Sunday School. "Oh be careful little eyes what you see. Oh, be careful little eyes what you see. For the Father up above is looking down in love. Oh, be careful little eyes what you see." We have control over what we choose to see. Sometimes we see things we would rather not have seen.

After having cataract surgery, it was exciting to see so well and clearly! We don't realize how poor our sight is until we get new glasses or contacts that bring our world into focus again. The sun is brighter, people's faces are clearer, and life just feels better.

We can anticipate heaven where all things are made clear both physically with our eyes and spiritually. All the questions we had on earth that we were going to ask when we got to heaven will be made clear to us without even asking. Some of the things we were concerned about on earth just won't matter when we get to heaven. God will have opened our eyes in a whole new way.

Hurry

"In repentance and rest is your salvation, in quietness and trust is your strength" (Isaiah 30:15).

Crocheting granny squares to make into lap robes is something I enjoy doing. I noticed when I am using up leftover yarn and not sure if I will have enough, I crochet faster. I'm not sure if I am afraid the rest of the yarn will run away from me or if it will stretch to last as long as needed. So the hurrier I go, the behinder I get! When I am getting close to finishing a prayer shawl, I find myself hurrying because I have five other ideas of what to make next. Knitting and crocheting should be something we do at leisure, not rushing to get finished. The longer we take to make a shawl, the more prayers are woven into it!

Isaiah 26:3 tells us, "You will keep in perfect peace him whose mind is steadfast, because he trusts in You." When we are in such a hurry to get things done, we miss the peace that God wants us to have. Isaiah goes on in 30:15, "In repentance and rest is your salvation, in quietness and trust is your strength." This is the true way to salvation and security. The verses following tell about fleeing on horses. In today's world, our cars are our horses. We flee down the road, passing everything that gets in our way, rushing to the next stop light before it turns yellow and have road rage when someone doesn't drive like we think they should. All to get to the next stop light and wait with the people we just passed. Are we in a hurry to get home to sit in our chair before it flies up off the floor without the weight of our body in it? Are we reflecting God's peace and our trust in God with this behavior?

Our neighbors, Jay and Glady, were elderly people and enjoyed us stopping in to visit. In the summer, they would have chairs on the front porch where we would sit awhile with them. There were cats winding around our feet and the dog needed a pat on the head. Jay and Glady didn't want us to bring them things as much as they enjoyed our time.

It's hard to get to know people if we are not willing to give them our time. The best gift you can give to others may be your time.

Psalm 119:59-60 tells us what we should hurry to do. "I have considered my ways and have turned my steps to your statutes. I will hasten and not delay to obey Your commands." It is God's law that fills the earth with all that makes life secure and joyous. We must hurry to obey God's law.

Zacchaeus was a short little man who climbed into a tree so he could see Jesus. Jesus noticed him up there and gave some specific orders. "When Jesus came by, he looked up a Zacchaeus and called him by name. 'Zacchaeus!' He said. 'Quick, come down! I must be a guest in your home today.' Zacchaeus quickly climbed down and took Jesus to his house in great excitement and joy." (NLT) Jesus expected immediate response and Zacchaeus was obedient. We don't know what the urgency was that this had to be done quickly, but Jesus spoke with urgency for him to hurry. When they got to his house, Jesus wanted to spend time with him.

Are we being discerning about when it is time to hurry and when we need to slow down? Ecclesiastes 3:1 tells us, "For everything there is a season, and a time for every matter under heaven." God gave us the freewill to know when we have to slow down and when it is time to hurry!

God's Names

"She will give birth to a son, and you are to give Him the name Jesus, because He will save His people from their sins" (Matthew 1:21).

Have you ever thought about all of God's names? The Christian community recognizes those names and realizes they are all biblical. People who are not Christian are confused by all the names that refer to our Lord. Below is a list of some of the names for God. There is a website that lists over 900 names of God if you are looking for a more extensive list. Read through them slowly and then claim the ones that are especially meaningful to you. Some people struggle with God as their Father, because their relationship with their earthly father is or was a painful relationship.

Rose of Sharon, Lily of the Valley, Friend, Redeemer, Savior, Father, Son of God, Lamb of God, Abba, Holy Ghost, Immanuel, Alpha, Omega, Comforter, Prince of Peace, Almighty God, Lord, Counselor, I Am, El Shaddai, Adonai, Yahweh, Elohim, Ancient of days, Author and finisher of our faith, Star of Jacob, Beloved Son, Bread of Life, Bridegroom, Bright and Morning Star, Teacher, and Good Shepherd.

While you are knitting or crocheting a prayer shawl, try to say a name of God for each stitch you make. If you work fast, it will be a challenge to come up with a new name to say! It challenges the brain and is a way to worship and pray while we knit or crochet. Or think of a name of God and contemplate that name for the row you are making. Thinking of Jesus as your friend and all the attributes that friendship brings to your relationship makes your heart full! It does mine!

We have one legal earthly name, but along the path of life we end up with nicknames. Some of them we take kindly to, but other names we get people to understand that we don't appreciate them. They can be hurtful and the tone of voice in which they are said speaks volumes to us. A pet name that our earthly father called us and it was said with love leaves a warm, fuzzy feeling of being loved. We may choose to not have others call us by that pet name. It is hard to control who calls us by what names. We need to be sensitive when we choose to call someone anything but their given name.

When parents are expecting a child, they will choose names for the baby. Then once the baby is here, they may decide that the name doesn't "fit" the baby. We think about that baby having that name for the rest of life and into eternity where God knows our name.

The Lord's Prayer has the phrase, "hallowed be Thy name" (Matthew 6:9). Jimmy Akin explain, "'Hallowed' is to do with the holiness of God. He argues that it is better to understand this line as 'may (or let) your name be holy.' When we pray this line, we are recognizing the nature of God as holy and distinct from us. This will lead us into a closer walk with our Creator and the development of holiness in ourselves, mirroring the nature of the God we worship."

Religious or Spiritual

"I know your deeds, that you are neither cold nor hot. I wish you were either one or the other. So, because you are lukewarm – neither hot nor cold – I am about to spit you out of my mouth" (Revelation 3:15-16).

This passage in Revelation is referring to the church of Laodicea that supplied neither healing for the spiritually sick nor refreshment for the spiritually weary. Laodicea was a very wealthy city that was widely known for its banking establishments, medical school and textile industry. The people felt their wealth would get them to heaven. They were "doing" religion to make it look good to the world. But God saw their heart and knew that it was "wretched, pitiful, poor, blind and naked" (verse 17).

We see a lot of people in our world who are very religious and are very dedicated in attending church, being seen in the right places, talk the talk but not necessarily walking the walk, doing good things for others and being a good person. But their spiritual life is very shallow or nonexistent. The spiritual life has been compared to riding on a train. There are people in different cars and as they mature in their spiritual life they move forward to different cars. Others stay in the same car or move further back as their spiritual life is stagnant or they stray away from the Good Shepherd.

Our spiritual lives need to be growing. Like a plant in the garden, it is either living or dying. There is no sort of living or sort of dying. For our spiritual lives to be healthy, we need to keep feeding on God's Word, be part of a spiritual community that includes spending time with fellow believers that challenge us to grow in our Spiritual lives. We can't "sort of" make a prayer shawl. Either we are making one or we aren't. While we are knitting or crocheting, we are spending time with our Lord. Part of our spiritual life should include attending a Bible teaching church, but that doesn't make you a Christian any more than standing in a garage makes you a car. We need to be listening, learning and growing from what is being said.

Evaluate your life to see if you are spiritually alive and growing or if you are stagnating in your religion. God knows your heart and longs to have you growing in Him.

A "Can Do" Attitude

"But because my servant Caleb has a different spirit and follows me wholeheartedly, I will bring him into the land he went to, and his descendants will inherit it" (Numbers 14:24).

Twelve men, representing the twelve tribes of Israel, had just come back from looking over the land of Canaan. Only Caleb and Joshua came back with positive reports that encouraged the people that they could conquer the land. Caleb's name means dog. Think of the joy, happiness, submissiveness and unconditional love a dog gives to its master. A dog follows its master wholeheartedly. Caleb is described here as "follows me wholeheartedly" and again in Joshua 14:8, "I, however, followed the Lord my God wholeheartedly." It wasn't until 45 years later that Caleb received his reward of his choice of land in Canaan when he was 85 years old.

Are we known for our "different spirit" that follows God wholeheartedly? This brings to mind the wife of noble character from Proverbs 31:10-31. She has that "can do" spirit who shows us wisdom and is "worth far more than rubies." When we are presented with a new idea or a challenging project, do we take on the challenge? When choosing a new knitting or crochet project, do you go with the old favorite, tried and tested pattern? If you are a "Caleb," you will take on a challenging, harder pattern. Take on the challenge of a pattern that is marked for intermediate or advanced knitters or crocheters! We need to start and finish something with a positive attitude, not a defeated spirit.

I worked for several years at an obstetrics and gynecology office. There were several doctors in that office, but I was drawn to one who had a very positive, Christian attitude. She was balancing a young family, marriage and a work schedule that required being on call for weekends and nights to deliver babies. When I had to have surgery done, it was an easy choice to have her be my surgeon. What peace I experienced that I was in her capable hands that were being held by our Heavenly Father's hands. I appreciated her sense of humor, her "can do" attitude that this surgery could be done and I would do well.

Making shawls is one challenge we can personally take on. Getting shawls to hurting people is also a challenge. In a large church, we are reaching out to many people that we don't know. It is important that all the members of the prayer shawl ministry are willing to reach out to hurting people. Frequently, someone in the group will know the person or a relative who can get the shawl to that hurting person. We are all members of one body!

Our "can do" attitude is our witness to the world. Our life and attitude may be the only Jesus some people will ever see.

And It Came to Pass

Have you ever thought about how often it says in the Bible "and it came to pass"? It is used 396 times in the King James Version. It usually refers to something that is going to happen or be fulfilled. It is not something that came to stay. This too shall pass away! Many times in life we have difficult, painful, uncomfortable situations, but when we think about it, that situation did not come to stay, it too passed. Many of these trials are brought on by decisions we make for ourselves. We do have difficult times in life that don't pass on. The diagnosis of a life threatening disease and tragic accidents that claim the life of loved ones are examples of life-altering situations where we do have to adjust our lives differently. We know God is there with us, but it feels like He is out of reach right then. The loss of a job may lead to a much better job or betrayal of a friend may lead to better understanding and other friends.

Psalm 23:4 tells us, "Even though I walk THROUGH the valley of the shadow of death, I will fear no evil." God doesn't bring us there to leave us, He walks through it with us where "Your rod and Your staff, they comfort me." He doesn't just walk us through the difficult time, He also is there to comfort and help us.

In Luke 22:28-32, Jesus shares with us about His trials. "You are those who have stood by me in my trials. And I confer on you a kingdom, just as my Father conferred one on me, so that you may eat and drink at my table in my kingdom and sit on thrones, judging the twelve tribes of Israel. Simon, Simon, Satan has asked to sift you as wheat. But I have prayed for you, Simon, that your faith may not fail. And when you have turned back, strengthen

59

your brothers." Jesus, our perfect example, faced severe trials. But they passed. He knew as each trial faced Him that, "It came to pass." Peter also faced trials, but they came to pass, just as Jesus had said they would. The trials passed and Peter became a better man because of them! As my maternal grandmother would say, "Life goes on with its trials and tribulations."

James 1:1-4 tells us, "James, a servant of God and of the Lord Jesus Christ, to the twelve tribes scattered among the nations: Greetings. Consider it pure joy, my brother, whenever you face trials of many kinds, because you know that the testing of your faith develops perseverance. Perseverance must finish its work so that you may be mature and complete, not lacking anything." James was also aware that when trials or temptations come, "It came to pass."

The people who receive prayer shawls are going through difficult times in their life. Our shawls are made with prayers to reach out and help the hurting ones through difficult times in their life. It is a tangible thing that a hurting person can hold on to that reminder around their shoulders or on their laps that fellow Christians are bringing them before God Almighty's throne to guide and care for them as it has "come to pass."

Be Nice

"Don't repay evil for evil. Don't retaliate with insults when people insult you. Instead, pay them back with a blessing. That is what God has called you to do, and He will bless you for it" (I Peter 3:9 NLT).

There is a bumper sticker on many vehicles that says, "Be Nice." It is interesting that we need to be reminded to be nice when that should be our very core value as a Christian. In Luke 6:32, Jesus tells us, "If you love those who love you, what credit is that to you? Even 'sinners' love those who love them." The challenge for us as Christians is to love as Christ loves us. Sadly, our world has become very familiar with bullying among children as well as adults. Schools, the workplace, highways and even in churches are all seeing the bullies throw their weight around. The golden rule was given to us long ago by Jesus in Luke 6:31, "Do to others as you would have them do to you." Some people have altered that thought and say, "Do unto other before they do to you." That's great if you plan to surprise them and do something nice. Be the first in line to do or say something nice to someone.

"Mobbing" is becoming more common in the workplace. It is a group of people who show aggression against an individual. It may start as "bullying," but through pressure, perks, rumors and mounting fear, and criticizing the work that person is doing, bullying escalates to the group of people ganging up on a person or a group of people. A person may think that everything they do is wrong, but they are the receiver of the mobbing. Frequently, this is a way that management uses to eliminate a worker.

People that are being bullied or mobbed feel they have nowhere to go or dare to confide or talk to anyone about the problem. They reach out for help to their parents, teachers, managers, pastors, and counselors. Depression sets in and some become so desperate they take their own life. One of the most effective ways to deal with this is to remove yourself from that environment. Children attending school in that environment need parental and teacher support to manage their way through this.

Words of encouragement, a smile, a cheerful greeting and an understanding, listening ear are some of the ways we can be nice! We can give prayer shawls to those we are aware of who need encouragement. Praying for those hurting in our world is a gift we can do for many people as we "pray without ceasing."

Yarn Reproducing

"Here is a boy with five small barley loaves and two small fish, but how far will they go among so many?" (John 6:9)

Are you aware that yarn reproduces in your closet or cupboard when you aren't looking? It doesn't seem to matter what color, brand or kind of yarn, it just reproduces! You can keep taking yarn out of the cupboard and get it made into something and when you go back to the cupboard there is more yarn there than when you last looked! Are there little sheep in the cupboard that lose their wooly coats and that gets made into yarn while the door is closed? Somehow it gets dyed to many colors, wound in skeins and a nice paper label wrapped around it. The paper always seems to have the brand that you like to buy and in colors you enjoy working with. Ahh, job security in making prayer shawls!

In John 6:5-13, we read the story of Jesus feeding 5,000 people with just five loaves of bread and two fish. Just like the yarn seems to reproduce, Jesus really made the five loaves and two fish reproduce. Jesus asks His men how much food they have. He tells them to go and find out. We know from John's account that all the food available in that vast crowd was the small lunch of a young boy. All he had was "five loaves and two fish." The loaves were not big, long loaves of bread. Rather, they were small round pieces of flatbread about the same size as a biscuit. The fish were not trophy bass or fifteen-pound Lake Michigan King salmon, they were the salted fish that the people of that area ate. They were about the size of sardines. When they returned with that small amount, the disciples expressed even more doubt. He says, "What are they among so many?" These fellows have sized up the crowd and the provisions and they have decided that there just isn't enough to go around. And, from a human perspective, they are right!

In Mark 6:39, He commands the people to sit down in groups or "companies." This word literally means "In rows like vegetables in a garden." Jesus has the people sit down in orderly rows. Their colorful garments making them look like a garden in bloom. That little tidbit doesn't add much to our understanding of the text, but it does remind us that our God is a God of order!

The women and children ate separately from the men. So the number 5,000 is just counting the men. So think of how much more food it took to feed the women and children as well! Jesus just kept breaking up the bread and fish and handing it out. And He didn't run out until all the people were fed.

When the people had finished eating, Jesus commanded the disciples to pick up the leftovers and they came back with twelve baskets full. One basket for each doubting disciple! Our "leftovers" of yarn can be gathered up and used as well. Granny squares are dear to my heart and I love putting the colors together to create them and then put the squares all together to make a lap robe. There are lots of uses for "leftover" yarn! Hats and mittens are always welcomed by children and their parents.

Jesus is the Lord of the Little! He took a little and made a lot out of it! He's still doing that! If you have a "little" situation you need to bring to Him, now would be a good time. And just enjoy the "never ending" supply of yarn that He has given you!

"In My Father's house are many rooms; if it were not so, I would have told you. I am going there to prepare a place for you" (John 14:2).

When we look at our supply of yarn, it looks like we plan to be on earth a long time to get that all knitted or crocheted! We talk about how we don't want our families to have to deal with all this "stuff" after we are gone. If only God would give us 30 days' notice before He calls us home to get these things in order. Give the treasures to people we know will appreciate them, get the stuff to the thrift stores that need to go there and put our house in order.

The song, "This world is not my home" an African-American Spiritual puts it in perspective for us.

This world is not my home, I'm just a passing through.
My treasures are laid up, somewhere beyond the blue.
The angels beckon me from heaven's open door.
And I can't feel at home in this world anymore.

O Lord, you know, I have no friend like you.
If heaven's not my home, O Lord what will I do.
The angels beckon me from heaven's open door.
And I can't feel at home in this world anymore.

These aging, decrepit bodies of ours are not our permanent ones! In II Corinthians 5:1 (NLT), we are told, "For we know that when this earthly tent we live in is taken down (that is, when we die and leave this earthly body), we will have a house in heaven, an eternal body made for us by God Himself and not by human hands." A tent is a temporary, flimsy place to live. Our bodies are frail, vulnerable and wasting away. Our heavenly body will be a permanent solid structure. It is built by God so it is perfect. I have some requests that I would like to make for my heavenly body! Thin, good eyesight, long flowing hair, thin, perfect teeth, no joint pain, did I mention that I would like to be thin?

We can live in anticipation of heaven and perfect bodies, but God wants us here on earth to live and thrive here. We can't just sit around and wait for Jesus to come or to call us home. He wants us to be working to further His kingdom while we wait for Him. Colossians 3:23 tells us, "Whatever you do, work at it with all your heart, as working for the Lord, not for men."

We keep on with our daily lives until Jesus comes. Making and giving prayer shawls is one way to reach out to hurting people while we wait for Jesus' perfect time to return or take us to Him.

Where is Your Mission Field?

The first time Bruce and Sherma attended our church, Sherma visited the ladies' room before finding a place to sit in the sanctuary. While she was in the stall doing her private thing, she hears a man's voice. She then realizes it was coming over the speaker system from in the sanctuary where they were practicing for the service. She almost wondered if it was God's voice speaking to her! A couple years later, she was again in the ladies' room and she started talking to Linda. Linda had attended our church for a short time and was looking to get connected. Sherma asked if she liked to knit or crochet, and Linda said she enjoyed knitting and had lots of yarn and time. So Sherma told her about the Prayer Shawl ministry and invited her to attend.

So where is your mission field? Is it in the church bathroom, the yarn aisle at Walmart or at a garage sale where there is lots of yarn for sale? It is amazing what conversations can start when people ask what you are going to make with the yarn. It opens the door for many people to ask about the prayer shawl ministry. For some people, it is a whole new concept, praying while knitting or crocheting.

I never liked to sing the song, "I'll Go Where You Want Me to Go" in Sunday school when I was growing up, because I was afraid God would send me to Africa and I really didn't want to go there. What a blessing to have a ministry doing what we enjoy and are able to reach out to hurting people as well as share the gospel with them. We can grow spiritually when we are praying while making the shawls and ministering to many hurting people with our finished shawls. God knows our likes and dislikes as well as our gifts and talents.

Before Jesus' death and resurrection, the gospel was to be proclaimed to the Jews only. Matthew 10:6 says, "Go rather to the lost sheep of Israel." Then in Matthew 28:19-20, which is after Jesus' death and resurrection, we are given the Great Commission, "Therefore go and make disciples of all nations, baptizing them in the name of the Father and of the Son and of the Holy Spirit, and teaching them to obey everything I have commanded you. And surely I am with you always, to the very end of the age." Baptizing was a sign of their union with and commitment to Christ. Jesus didn't say, "Come and sit," He said, "Go and do!"

We may feel inadequate in sharing the gospel. Just remember, God doesn't call the qualified, He qualifies the called. He will give you the wisdom and the words to say.

Same Old, Same Old

"The Israelites ate manna forty years, until they came to a land that was settled; they ate manna until they reached the border of Canaan" (Exodus 16:35).

We may criticize the Israelites for grumbling about what they didn't have to eat or drink and then they grumbled about what they did have to eat and drink. God provided manna for them, literally dropping it from the sky along with quail for meat. Have you considered how many ways you can prepare manna, three times a day? If you think of your favorite food and then consider eating that three times a day for forty years. I doubt that we could do that for three to four days. Sounds to me like SSDD – same stuff, different day! Earlier in Chapter 16, they complained to Moses about no food and then wished for the food they had in Egypt. They conveniently forgot about the slavery and the abuse they endured there. God used that time in the desert to instruct and mature the people He had called to follow Him.

Sometimes I will make two prayer shawls from the same color and same pattern (have to use up the yarn, you know). By the end of the second shawl, I am very tired of the pattern and the colors. Imagine always using the same pattern and the same colors on every shawl you make.

Lamentations 3:22-23 tells us, "Because of the Lord's great love we are not consumed, for His compassions never fail. They are new every morning, great is Your faithfulness." Every morning, the Israelites had a new supply of manna, except for

Sunday and God had given them instructions to pick up enough on the sixth day to last through the seventh day. So new manna every morning is just like God's faithfulness is new every morning of our lives.

Where Is Your Bible?

"I have hidden Your word in my heart that I might not sin against You" (Psalm 119:11).

My paternal grandparents had a special little shelf within reach of the kitchen table where the Bible was kept. When they finished eating, Grandpa reached for the Bible and read scripture and then closed with prayer. That Bible had brown paper neatly folded around the cover to protect it. I never have seen the cover of that Bible! I grew up in a home where the same routine was followed.

Where is your Bible? I have a girlfriend who has it under her chair in the living room so she can reach for it while she is sitting there. One man was moving from one house to another and most of his possessions were put in storage for a while. His Bible was also put in storage. I ask again, where is your Bible? Psalm 119:105 tells us, "Your word is a lamp to my feet and a light for my path." It's pretty hard for us to use the Bible for a lamp when it is in the drawer.

In Deuteronomy 11:18-19, God asks us to "Fix these words of Mine in your hearts and minds; tie them as symbols on your hands and bind them on your foreheads. Teach them to your children, talking about them when you sit at home and when you walk along the road, when you lie down and when you get up." God wants His words in our hearts so we have them for recall when we don't have access to a Bible. In verse 20, God instructs them to, "Write them on the doorframes of your houses and on your gates." If a stranger walks into your house, is there any

71

indication in the décor that a Christian lives there? Do the pictures on the walls proclaim who is the head of your household? With all the sayings on shirts that we wear, do they proclaim Jesus lives in your heart?

Shirley Rice tells us, "How much of a calm and gentle spirit you achieve, then, will depend on how regularly and consistently, persistently and obediently you partake of the Word of God, your spiritual food." Sometimes we need to lay down our needles and hooks and pick up the Bible to feed our souls. We should not drain ourselves dry giving to others and not feed and nourish our spiritual appetites. We won't have anything to give to others if we are spiritually dry ourselves. Colossians 3:16 encourages us to, "Let the Word of Christ dwell in you richly as you teach and admonish one another with all wisdom, and as you sing psalms, hymns and spiritual songs with gratitude in your hearts to God." It is easier for me to remember scripture with the songs that put verses to music. Listening to Christian music puts those words in my heart. Then when I wake in the morning, a song is in my heart and the words speak to me.

42179701R00043

Made in the USA
Middletown, DE
03 April 2017